STEP ONE: TEACH YOURSELF VIOLIN

DVD Edition

Cover photography by Randall Wallace

This book Copyright © 2009 by Amsco Publications,
A Division of Music Sales Corporation, New York

Order No. AM983587
International Standard Book Number: 978-0-8256-3450-5

Exclusive Distributors:
Music Sales Corporation
257 Park Avenue South, New York, NY 10010 USA
Music Sales Limited
14-15 Berners Street, London W1T 3LJ England
Music Sales Pty. Limited
20 Resolution Drive, Caringbah, NSW 2229, Australia

Printed in the United States of America by
Vicks Lithograph and Printing Corporation

Amsco Publications
New York/London/Paris/Sydney/Copenhagen/Berlin/Tokyo/Madrid

Contents

Introduction 5

Basics of Music Notation 6

Equipment 8

Holding the Violin 9

Tuning 10

Open Strings 11

Practice Time 14

    On the Bridge 15

    Hänsel and Gretel 15

    Moonlight 16

    Acres of Clams 17

    Go Tell Aunt Rhody 18

    Yankee Doodle 19

    The Wabash Cannonball 19

Fiddle and Violin 20

    Twinkle, Twinkle 20

    Bile 'Em Cabbage 20

    Turkey in the Straw 21

    Liberty 22

    Camptown Races 22

    French Lullaby 23

    Streets of Laredo 24

    Freré Jacques 24

    Jingle Bells 25

    Dona 26

    O Come All Ye Faithful 27

    The Battle Hymn of the Republic 27

    Rondeau 28

    William Tell Overture 28

    Love Theme from H.M.S. Pinafore 29

    Minuet 30

    Minuet 30

Epilogue 31

Introduction

So you've dreamed of playing the violin but are a little afraid to get started. Well, with a little study and practice, anyone can play violin—and this proven violin method will get you started. This easy, step-by-step method will guide you through all the basics of violin performance and technique. As with every new hobby, it will take some time at first to get the hang of the basics. But once they are under your fingers, so to speak, you'll be able to launch yourself into the exciting new world of the violin.

Of course, playing the violin is a continuously evolving experience. Those who have played for years are still learning everyday. But for the beginning violinist, although the challenges of the instrument can be frustrating at first, they can also be immensely rewarding.

This comprehensive violin method is easy and fun—and does not rely on tricks and shortcuts that only work for certain songs in certain keys. On the contrary, you can learn to play a variety of violin music and develop all the skills you need to learn hundreds of new songs on your own after you finish the method.

Chord symbols are included with each tune so that the accompaniment can be played by a teacher, parent or friend. This will help keep you in tune and make the whole learning process more enjoyable.

Whether you intend to be a professional violinist or simply wish to play for your community, family, and friends—this book is for you. So, get ready to learn the basics of violin as you play some of the world's most popular melodies.

Basics of Music Notation

Here are some basics of music notation:

whole note	=	𝅝	whole rest	=	▬	or	4 beats
half note	=	𝅗𝅥	half rest	=	▬	or	2 beats
quarter note	=	♩	quarter rest	=	𝄽	or	1 beat
eight note	=	♪	eight rest	=	𝄾	or	½ beat
sixteenth note	=	𝅘𝅥𝅯	sixteenth rest	=	𝄿	or	¼ beat

A whole note is equivalent to 2 half notes, 4 quarter notes, 8 eighth notes, *etc.*
In other words:

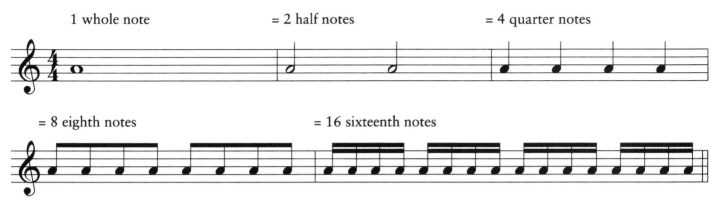

1 whole note   = 2 half notes   = 4 quarter notes

= 8 eighth notes   = 16 sixteenth notes

The rhythm is different yet the time taken up is the same.

A *dot* next to the note (♩.) indicates that one-half of that note's value is to be added to the duration of that note.

For example:

$$𝅗𝅥. = 𝅗𝅥 + ♩$$

$$♩. = ♩ + ♪$$

$$♪. = ♪ + 𝅘𝅥𝅯$$

The same principle applies to rests.

$$▬. = ▬ + 𝄽$$

$$𝄽. = 𝄽 + 𝄾$$

$$𝄾. = 𝄾 + 𝄿$$

Other basics:

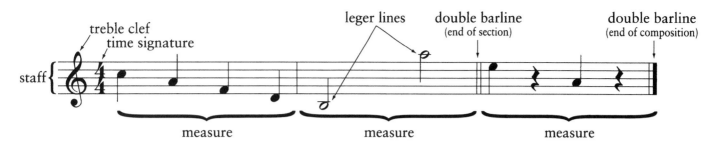

Staff: The five lines and four spaces on which the musical language of notes and symbols are arranged.

Treble clef: Also called the G clef, provides a frame of reference for notes placed on the lines and spaces of the staff.

Leger lines: The additional lines used to extend the staff.

Time signature: This symbol indicates two important facts about the overall rhythm of the piece. The top number indicates the number of beats per measure and the bottom number indicates the value of the beat.

Barline: The vertical lines that divide the music on the staff into sections called *measures*.

Double barline: Two thin lines indicates the end of a musical section. One thin line and one thick line indicated the end of the composition.

Accidentals: Symbols used to alter a pitch; a flat (♭) lowers the pitch one half step, a sharp (♯) raises the pitch one half step, and a natural (♮) returns the pitch to its unaltered state.

Slurs: A curved line connecting two or more notes which calls for them to be played smoothly. You should play all of these notes with the same bow stroke.

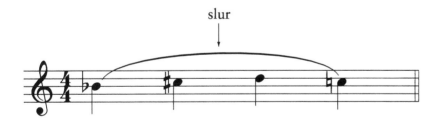

Throughout the book there will be more development and explanation of these and other musical terms.

Equipment

The first aspect of playing the violin is, obviously, getting a violin (and don't forget the bow). There is an enormous price range for violins, from a couple hundred dollars to hundreds of thousands and beyond. Realistically, a good beginner violin and bow can be found for approximately one hundred dollars. There really isn't any real need to spend more at this juncture. Violins come in different sizes and it's best to go to your local music store to ask which size is appropriate for you. Usually by the age of thirteen or fourteen a full size violin is manageable. These diagrams will show you the violin and bow, with the names to all the parts.

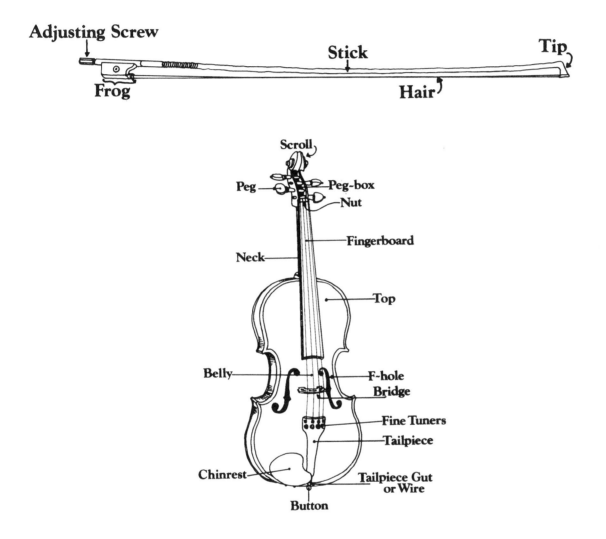

Along with the violin and bow, you will want to obtain these key accessories: rosin, shoulder rest, and extra strings. When applied to the bow hair, rosin creates the friction with the strings which in turn generates the sound. You'll need to use a knife to scrape the top of the rosin in several places so that the powder appears. Then run the bow hair over it until you see the hair getting whiter. The shoulder rest gets affixed under the violin to make holding the violin easier (see the next section). It is also a good idea to have extra strings. Strings should be changed every three to five months with the help of a teacher or more experienced player.

Holding the Violin

A very important aspect of learning the violin is developing an awareness of your body in relation to the violin. Always try to stay as relaxed as possible. If you feel your shoulders, neck, or hands tensing up then take a deep breath, relax that area, and go back to that position. Once you are standing comfortably, lift the violin to your left shoulder. The chin rest should go under your left jaw line and the bottom of your violin against the collarbone. Many people use a shoulder rest, which serves two purposes. First, it increases the depth of the violin so that there is a nice snug fit without tensing your neck, and second, it provides cushioning for the collarbone. Try to hold the violin up without the use of your left arm. This skill will become more important as your level rises.

Now take the bow with your right hand. Place your thumb between the stick and the hair at the frog.

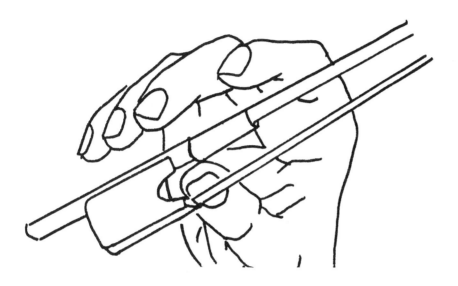

Your fingers should be evenly placed on top of the stick with your pinky near the adjusting screw. Remember to stay as relaxed as possible. This will help to make your bowing freer, easier and less tiring. In addition, tighten the bow hair so that there is some tension before you start playing and loosen it after you've stopped playing.

Tuning

The violin's four strings are tuned to G, D, A, E.

Tuning the violin can be tricky at first. Here are some ways to do it yourself.

A tuning fork or pitch pipe will give you the proper pitch. Tuning forks are commonly set to A=440, which is the same A as the violin's second string. Therefore using the peg and fine tuners, adjust the pitch of the string until it is the same as that of the tuning fork. A pitch pipe will give you all of the pitches, so repeat the process for the other strings. A piano or electronic tuner can also be used.

Open Strings

Now, get your violin in position and let's play. We'll start with just open strings to get used to the feel of the instrument. Placing the bow midway between the bridge and the fingerboard will give you an optimal sound. With a firm, yet supple hand, pull the bow down trying to keep the bow at a right angle to the strings. Then back up the same way. The pulling motion is indicated by a ⊓ and the up bow stroke by a ∨. You may find that practicing in front of a mirror can be valuable. By keeping the wrist flexible on the bow changes, your tone will eventually stay smooth and strong.

Use a long bowing motion, back and forth. Repeat the note until you feel you are consistently generating good tone.

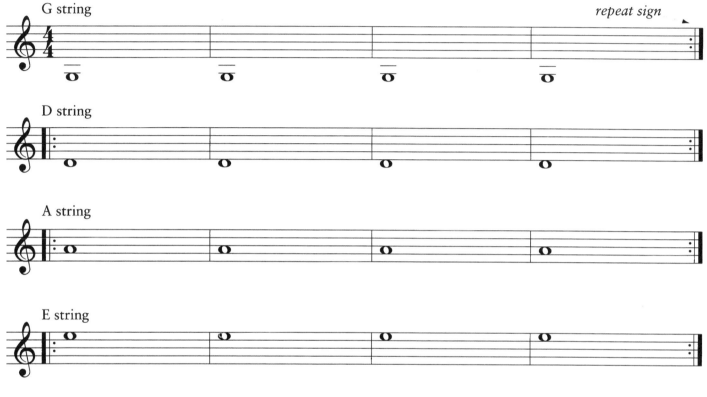

Now, let's accelerate the bow just a little bit. First with half-notes, and then with quarter-notes.

The next exercises relate to rhythm as well. Try them on all strings.

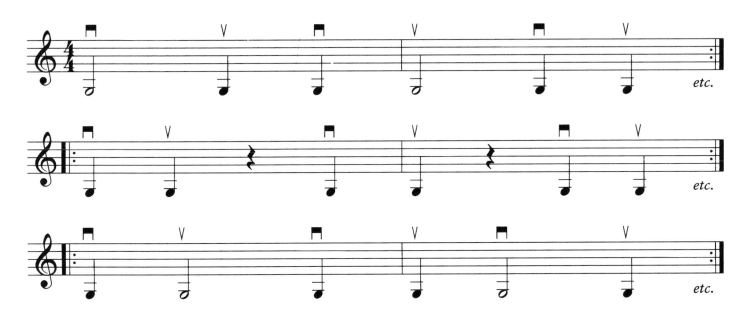

Now, we're going to get a feel for switching strings. The key is to have as clean a switch as possible. That means that the timing between the change of direction and the string switch must be synchronized.

Once you have the hang of the open strings we can then take a look at some scales. Scales represent the notes contained in a given key. Let's start out in the key of G, that means that a piece in that key will be made up of primarily the same notes in the scale.

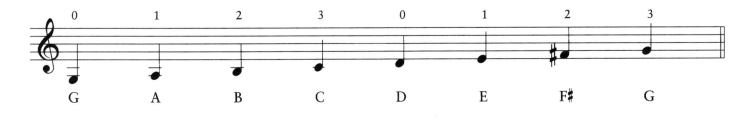

The key of G contains one sharp: F♯.

You can also play a G scale one octave higher.

Many pieces of music require that certain notes be sharped or flatted as a general rule. The number of *accidentals* (sharps or flats) that occur regularly in a piece of music determines the key. Rather than writing in a sharp or flat sign every time one should occur, these signs are written in a key signature at the beginning of each staff.

The *time signature* is made up of two numbers. The bottom number represents the duration of the beats and the top number represents the amount of those beats per measure. Therefore, ¾ means three quarter notes per measure. Some common time signatures are ¾, ⁴⁄₄, and ⁶⁄₈.

One last exercise before we get to the pieces. This one combines string crossing with fingering.

Practice Time

People have different levels of commitments as well as time, so in general, practice time will be an individual choice. The key to practicing is quality over quantity. If you can only commit to twenty minutes every other day or can practice up to an hour a day, the principles are the same: Make every minute count. At the beginner level, it is often more beneficial to practice efficiently for small bursts of time. Even five to ten minutes of intense concentration on the scales and exercises, and then the same on a couple of pieces, is reasonable. Always make sure that good tone, smooth bow, relaxed body and the other basics are attained.

This simple tune is a nice way to start playing a piece. There are very few intervallic jumps, so try to play as cleanly as possible.

This next piece is a very popular children's song in France.

On the Bridge

The next example introduces *alternate endings* in the first half of the piece. A bracket and a numeral is used in these instances to mark the measure or measures of each different ending. This means that you should skip the first ending on the repeat and go to the second ending before moving on to the next section.

Hänsel and Gretel

We now move on to the key of D.

Here's another French tune.

Moonlight

France

This one was originally called "Rosin, the Beau" in Ireland, but in America it took on a new name.

Acres of Clams

United States

Here is the A scale in two different octaves.

These next three tunes are all traditional American melodies.

Go Tell Aunt Rhody

United States

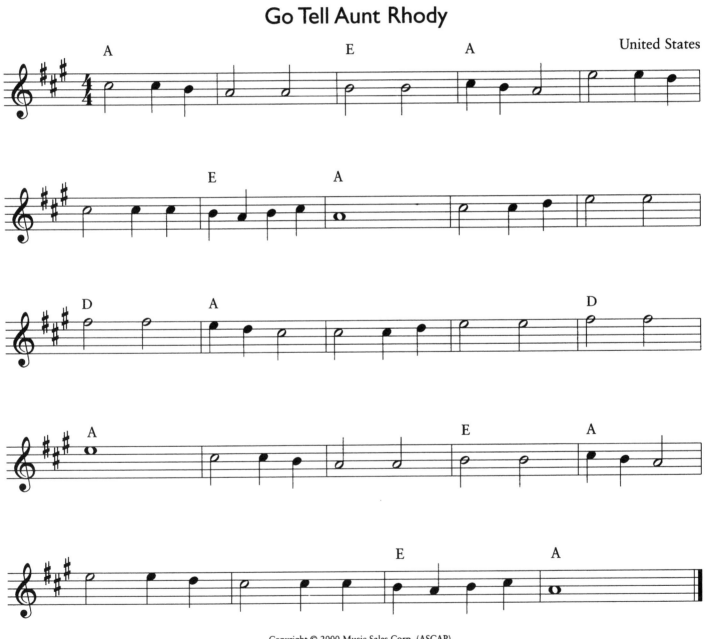

Yankee Doodle

United States

The Wabash Cannonball

United States

Fiddle and Violin

One of the most common questions that violinists get is what's the difference between a fiddle and a violin? The answer of course is nothing! The words only refer to styles of music, violin to classical, and fiddle to, well, almost anything else. The whole genre of fiddle music encompasses everything from Irish to Appalachian to Bluegrass styles. But fiddle music and classical violin music are related.

Fiddle music usually is a specific dance style: jigs, waltzes, etc. For example, if you were to look at some of the greatest classical music, say Bach, you'd find that he uses jigs, waltzes, and all sorts of other dances as the foundation for much of his music.

Here is an example of how similar a simple classical tune and a simple fiddle tune can be.

Twinkle, Twinkle

W.A. Mozart (1756–1791)

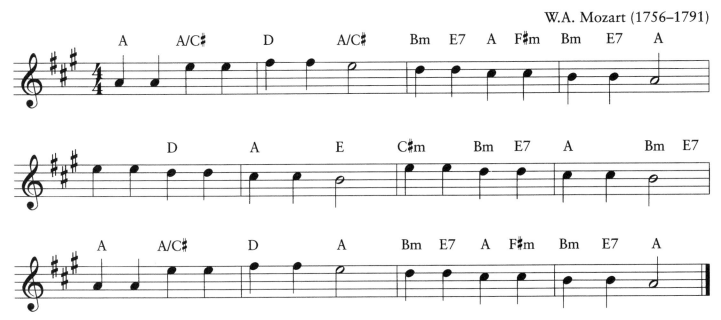

Bile 'Em Cabbage

Traditional

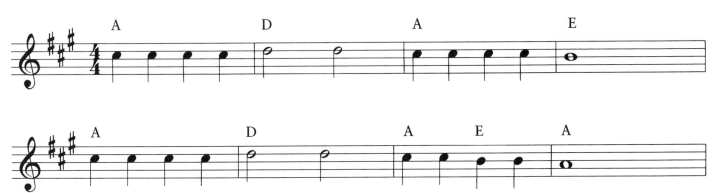

Here are three more fiddle tune favorites.

Turkey in the Straw

Traditional

Liberty

Traditional

Camptown Races

Stephen Foster (1826–1864)

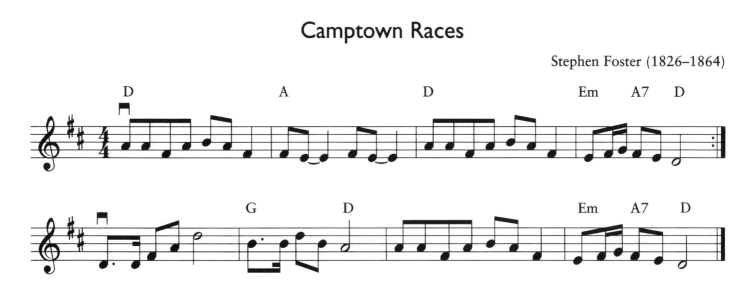

And the same holds true for these two waltzes.

French Lullaby

Traditional

Streets of Laredo

For many of these pieces, the key in which they are played is not so important to the integrity of the music. As an example, notice how the French round "Frère Jacques" works equally well in three different keys: G, D, and A.

Freré Jacques

Finally, let's look at some pieces that are a little more involved. Everybody's Christmas favorite, "Jingle Bells," is significantly longer than the previous pieces, so it will be a good way to test your stamina.

Jingle Bells

James S. Pierpont (1822–1893)

Below is the D minor scale. Notice that the key signature has one flat (B♭).

D minor scale

Now try playing this traditional Jewish melody in D minor.

Dona

Traditional Jewish

This well-known Christmas hymn has a gorgeous melody,

O Come All Ye Faithful

Tradtional English carol

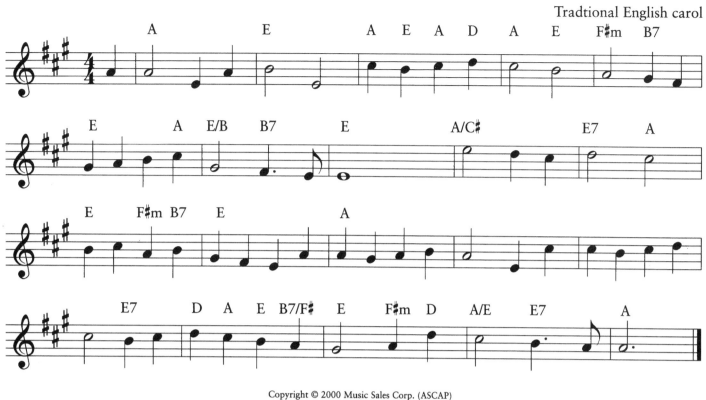

Watch out for the dotted rhythms in this patriotic classic.

The Battle Hymn of the Republic

Julia Ward Howe (1819–1910)

Fans of public television may recognize this next piece as the "Theme from Masterpiece Theater."

Rondeau

Jean-Joseph Mouret (1682–1738)

While fans of classic television will remember this one as the Lone Ranger's theme.

William Tell Overture

Gioacchino Rossini (1792–1868)

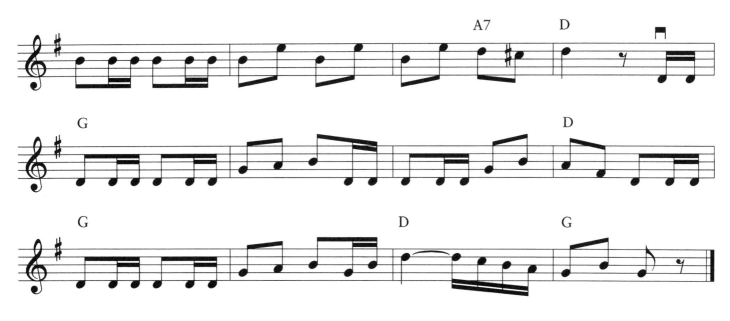

This beautiful waltz was very popular at the end of the nineteenth century.

Love Theme from H.M.S. Pinafore

Sir Arthur Sullivan (1842–1900)

Remember that Bach used dances as the foundation for much of his music? Minuets were an extremely popular form of dancing for several hundred years.

Minuet

J.S. Bach (1685–1750)

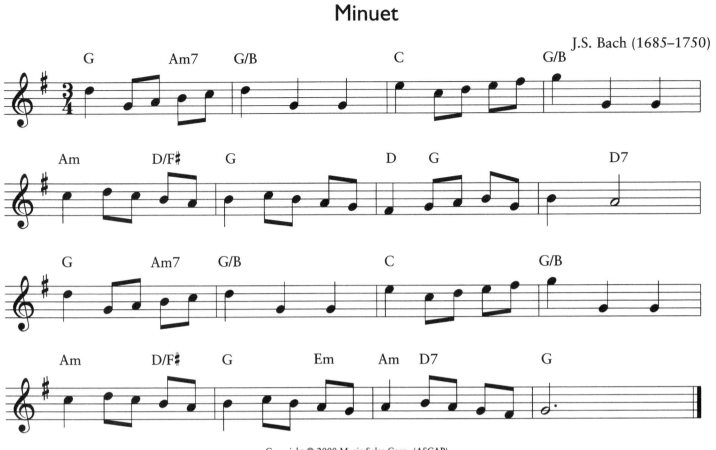

Mozart also used the form. Notice that minuets are in ¾ time.

Minuet

W.A. Mozart (1756–1791)

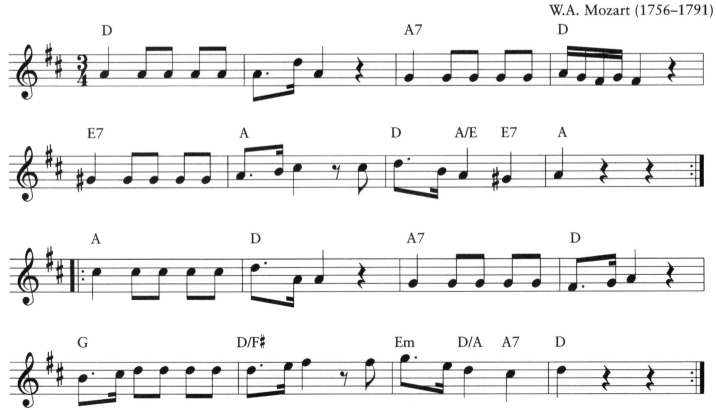

Epilogue

This book is only scratching the surface of the world of the violin. Even the most accomplished player has more to learn. There are many more keys to become familiar with, techniques to master, and styles of music to discover. Hopefully, this book has given you a good start and piqued your interest.

Remember that one of the most important aspects of learning is human contact. The interchange of ideas and advice with a more experienced player or teacher is invaluable.

So, good luck and remember to have fun.